CREEK

Big Buddy Books
An Imprint of Abdo Publishing
www.abdopublishing.com

Sarah Tieck

www.abdopublishing.com

Published by Abdo Publishing, a division of ABDO, PO Box 398166, Minneapolis, Minnesota 55439.
Copyright © 2015 by Abdo Consulting Group, Inc. International copyrights reserved in all countries. No part
of this book may be reproduced in any form without written permission from the publisher. Big Buddy Books™
is a trademark and logo of Abdo Publishing.

Printed in the United States of America, North Mankato, Minnesota.
102014
012015

Cover Photo: © NativeStock.com/Angel Wynn; Shutterstock.com.
Interior Photos: *Getty Images*: DEA/G. DAGLI ORTI/Contributor (p. 15), MPI/Stringer (pp. 17, 26), Science &
    Society Picture Library/Contributor (p. 23), J. Vespa (p. 30), The Washington Post/Contributor (p. 29);
    © NativeStock.com/Angel Wynn (pp. 5, 9, 13, 16, 17, 19, 25, 27); Shutterstock.com (pp. 11, 21).

Coordinating Series Editor: Rochelle Baltzer
Contributing Editors: Bridget O'Brien, Marcia Zappa
Graphic Design: Adam Craven

Library of Congress Cataloging-in-Publication Data

Tieck, Sarah, 1976-
  Creek / Sarah Tieck.
      pages cm. -- (Native Americans)
  Audience: Ages 7-11.
  ISBN 978-1-62403-579-1
  1. Creek Indians--Juvenile literature. I. Title.
  E99.C9T54 2015
  975.004'97385--dc23
                               9635
                    2014030604

CONTENTS

AMAZING PEOPLE

Hundreds of years ago, North America was mostly wild, open land. Native American tribes lived on the land. They had their own languages and **customs**.

The Creek (KREEK) are one Native American tribe. They are known for their hunting skills and stomp dances. Let's learn more about these Native Americans.

Did You Know?

The name *Creek* came from British settlers. It was because the tribe lived along creeks. They called themselves *Muskogee*, which means "land that is wet or floods."

4

Creek families honor their history and way of life at festivals.

CREEK TERRITORY

Creek homelands were in what is now the southeastern United States. The Creek lived in the flatlands of present-day Georgia and Alabama.

There were Upper Creeks and Lower Creeks. Upper Creeks were also known as Muskogee. Lower Creeks were also called Hitchiti and Alabama. Upper and Lower Creeks shared **traditions** but spoke different forms of their language.

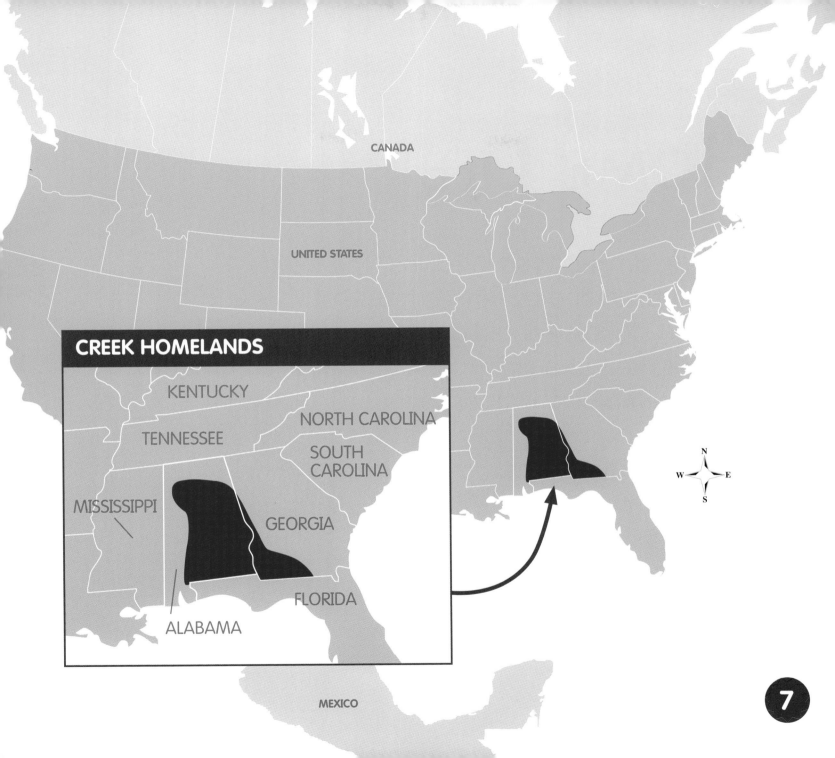

CREEK HOMELANDS

CANADA

UNITED STATES

KENTUCKY

NORTH CAROLINA

TENNESSEE

SOUTH
CAROLINA

MISSISSIPPI

GEORGIA

FLORIDA

ALABAMA

MEXICO

N
W E
S

HOME LIFE

Creek families lived in towns. The towns were surrounded by fences made of wooden stakes. People gathered in central squares. Round buildings in the squares held **ceremonies**. Homes were built around squares.

Creek homes were rectangular. Poles held up a roof made of bark or thatch. Sometimes, the homes had walls made of smaller poles covered with plaster. A hole in the roof let out smoke from fires.

A center square was also called a "stomp ground." Ceremonies, dances, and meetings took place there.

What They Ate

The Creek were skilled farmers. They grew vegetables such as corn, beans, and squash.

The Creek ate meat from the animals they hunted. To hunt deer, men painted their faces. They believed this improved their sight. They sang to bring the deer close.

The tribe also ate fish. Men used bows and arrows and special traps to catch fish.

Farming corn was a major part of Creek life.

Daily Life

Family groups called clans gathered in their town's central square. There were Wind, Bird, Alligator, and Bear clans.

The Creek wore decorated clothing. Women wore skirts. Men wore **loincloths** and sometimes leggings. Both men and women wore lots of decorations, such as feathers and beads. Some wore moccasins to **protect** their feet.

Creek families lived in compounds, or groups of buildings. These often included buildings for sleeping, cooking, and storage.

Creek moccasins were made from animal skins, such as deerskin.

In a Creek town, people had different jobs. Men hunted and fished. They were builders, warriors, and chiefs.

Women took care of the children and ran the homes. They tended gardens and made food. Children learned by helping and watching others in the community.

Creek warriors planned attacks when they needed to.

15

MADE BY HAND

The Creek made many objects by hand. They often used natural materials. These arts and crafts added beauty to everyday life.

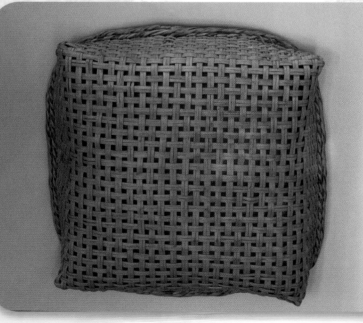

Baskets
The Creek wove basket trays from hickory trees. They were used to process food. The baskets were rarely decorated.

Tattoos

Creek men and women had elaborate tattoos. Some covered their entire bodies. The people also painted their bodies.

Pottery

Creek pottery was mostly used for cooking. Many pieces were decorated with scratches or carved lines.

Spirit Life

The Creek believed in a god called the Master of Breath. He lived above the sky. They took daily baths as part of their religion.

Throughout the year, the Creek held **ceremonies** and **rituals** in town squares. Sometimes, stomp dances were part of these events. The Green Corn Ceremony happened in summer. Many crimes and sins were forgiven at the event.

During stomp dances, women wore turtle shell rattles on their legs. Their movements helped set the beat.

STORYTELLERS

Stories are important to the Creek. Storytellers collect and remember legends and folktales. They share them to teach people about the tribe's **culture** and history.

The Creek tell stories about characters such as Rabbit, who is a trickster. Some stories are about battles between people and monsters. Others describe floods.

The Creek lived near water. So, it was often part of their stories.

FIGHTING FOR LAND

In 1539, the Creek met Spanish explorer Hernando de Soto and his men. Over time, the Spanish began to settle the land and build colonies.

The Creek were part of a group of tribes called the Creek Confederacy. It included the Yuchi, some Natchez, and other tribes. Together, they fought settlers and northern tribes. Still, settlement took away much of their land.

The style of Creek homes changed as settlers moved onto their land.

23

In the 1800s, the US government made the Creek give up some of their land. A group of Creek known as the Red Sticks fought back in the Creek War. Yet, they lost this war and much of their land.

In the 1830s, the US government forced the Creek to move to Indian Territory. This was in present-day Oklahoma. Today, some Creek use laws to **protect** their way of life. Many have built a good life and are living well.

Chief Menawa led the Red Sticks.

BACK IN TIME

1813

Many Creek joined Shawnee leader Tecumseh in the Creek War against the United States.

1539

The Creek met Spanish explorer Hernando de Soto and his men. They fought each other.

1814

The Battle of Horseshoe Bend took place. This ended the Creek War. The Creek lost more than half of their land.

1830s

Many Creek were forced to move to Indian Territory. This was called the Indian Removal Act.

1898

The Curtis Act was passed. This took apart the leadership of Native American nations, including the Creek. This followed the Dawes Act of 1887. Both laws weakened Native American tribes.

1970s

Some Creek set up a new tribal **constitution** and chose leaders.

THE CREEK TODAY

The Creek have a long, rich history. They are remembered for their decorated clothing and powerful fighters.

Creek roots run deep. Today, the people have kept alive those special things that make them Creek. Even though times have changed, many people carry the **traditions**, stories, and memories of the past into the present.

Did You Know?

In 2010, there were about 48,000 Creek in the United States.

Today, the Creek share their culture at events such as the American Indian Festival.

"My generation is now the door to memory. This is why I am remembering."

— Joy Harjo, Creek poet

GLOSSARY

ceremony a formal event on a special occasion.

constitution (kahnt-stuh-TOO-shuhn) the basic laws that govern a group of people.

culture (KUHL-chuhr) the arts, beliefs, and ways of life of a group of people.

custom a practice that has been around a long time and is common to a group or a place.

loincloth a simple cloth worn by a man to cover his lower body.

protect (pruh-TEHKT) to guard against harm or danger.

ritual (RIH-chuh-wuhl) a formal act or set of acts that is repeated.

tradition (truh-DIH-shuhn) a belief, a custom, or a story handed down from older people to younger people.

WEBSITES

To learn more about Native Americans, visit **booklinks.abdopublishing.com**. These links are routinely monitored and updated to provide the most current information available.

INDEX